spot

MIGHTY MACHINES

TOW TRUCKS

by Wendy Strobel Dieker

AMICUS | AMICUS INK

lights

hook

Look for these
words and pictures
as you read.

winch

wheel lift

Here comes a tow truck.
What can it do?

Tow trucks pull.
They are strong. They pull
broken cars and trucks.

See the flashing lights?
They are a warning.
Other cars stay back.

lights

See the hook?

It has a latch.

It hooks onto the car.

hook

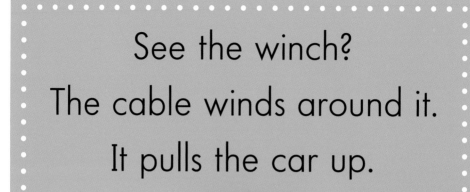

See the winch?
The cable winds around it.
It pulls the car up.

winch

See the wheel lift?
It lifts one end of a car.
The tow truck takes
the car away.

wheel lift

Tow trucks help keep roads safe.

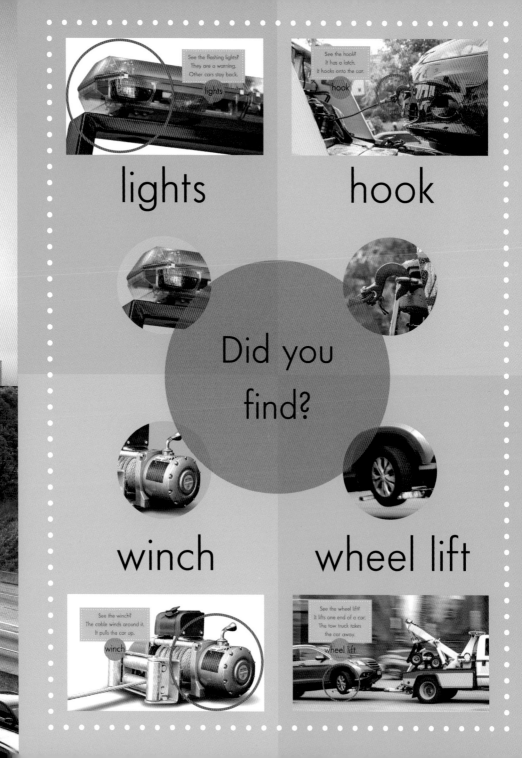

lights

hook

Did you find?

winch

wheel lift

spot

Spot is published by Amicus and Amicus Ink
P.O. Box 1329, Mankato, MN 56002
www.amicuspublishing.us

Library of Congress Cataloging-in-Publication Data
Names: Dieker, Wendy Strobel, author.
Title: Tow trucks / by Wendy Strobel Dieker.
Description: Mankato, Minnesota : Amicus, [2019] |
Series: Spot. Mighty machines | Audience: K to Grade 3.
Identifiers: LCCN 2017033370 (print) | LCCN 2017055760
 (ebook) | ISBN 9781681514598 (pdf) | ISBN 9781681513775
 (library binding) | ISBN 9781681522975 (pbk.)
Subjects: LCSH: Wreckers (Vehicles)--Juvenile literature. |
 CYAC: Wreckers (Vehicles).
Classification: LCC TL230.5.W74 (ebook) | LCC TL230.5.W74
 .D54 2019 (print) | DDC 629.225--dc23
LC record available at https://lccn.loc.gov/2017033370

Printed in China

HC 10 9 8 7 6 5 4 3 2 1
PB 10 9 8 7 6 5 4 3 2 1

To my favorite mighty machine
drivers, Big Jerr and Smoke 'em
Joe —WSD

Rebecca Glaser, editor
Deb Miner, series designer
Aubrey Harper, book designer
Holly Young, photo researcher

Photos by Alamy Stock Photo/
Stephen Barnes, 10-11; Flickr/
JOHN LLOYD, cover, 16;
Getty/Thinkstock, 6-7; iStock/
kozmoat98, 1, Jodi Jacobson,
3, Terryfic3D, 4-5, traveler1116,
14-15; Shutterstock/CC7, 8-9,
blurAZ, 12-13

TOW TRUCKS